MW01122021

Humber College Library
3199 Lakeshore Blvd. West
Toronto, ON   M8V 1K8

THE (POST) MISTRESS

Also by Tomson Highway

THE (POST)
MISTRESS

A One-Woman Musical

with book, lyrics, and music

by

TOMSON HIGHWAY

Talonbooks

HUMBER LIBRARIES LAKESHORE CAMPUS
3199 Lakeshore Blvd West
TORONTO, ON.   M8V 1K8

© 2013 by Tomson Highway

Talonbooks
P.O. Box 2076, Vancouver, British Columbia, Canada V6B 3S3
www.talonbooks.com

Typeset in Frutiger
Printed and bound in Canada on 100% post-consumer recycled paper
Cover photograph of Patricia Cano performing in the National Arts Centre
French Theatre production in October 2012
Cover photograph by Bryan McNally
Typeset and cover design by Typesmith

First printing: 2013

All rights reserved. No part of this book may be reproduced, stored in a
retrieval system, or transmitted, in any form or by any means, without
the prior written consent of the publisher or a licence from the Canadian
Copyright Licensing Agency (Access Copyright). For a copyright licence,
visit accesscopyright.ca or call toll free to 1-800-893-5777.

Talonbooks gratefully acknowledges the financial support of the Canada
Council for the Arts, the Government of Canada through the Canada Book
Fund, and the Province of British Columbia through the British Columbia
Arts Council and the Book Publishing Tax Credit.

Rights to produce *The (Post) Mistress*, in whole or in part, in any medium by
any group, amateur or professional, are retained by the author. Interested
persons are requested to apply to his agent: Catherine Mensour, L'Agence
Mensour Agency Ltd., 41 ch. Springfield Rd., Ottawa, Ontario K1M 1C8;
tel.: 613-241-1677; fax: 613-241-4360; e-mail: kate@mensour.ca.

For more information about the musical score and to purchase a recording
of songs and accompanying music, please visit the Talon website at www.
talonbooks.com.

Library and Archives Canada Cataloguing in Publication

Highway, Tomson, 1951–, author
    The (post) mistress / Tomson Highway.

Issued in print and electronic formats. ISBN 978-0-88922-780-4 (pbk.). –
ISBN 978-0-88922-781-1 (epub)

    I. Title.
PS8565.I433P67 2013   C812'.54   C2013-903574-5
                                               C2013-903575-3

Keetha kichi ooma masinaa-igan, Patricia Cano.
Athis ithigook eeneetaanagamooyin. Igwa ithigook
meena eek'seewaatsee-in. Kimshi-nanaaskoomitin

PRODUCTION HISTORY

The (Post) Mistress was first produced, in an earlier draft, at and by Magnus Theatre in Thunder Bay, Ontario, from January 27 to February 12, 2011, with the following cast and company:

The Postmistress	Pandora Topp
Pianist	Danny Johnson
Saxophonist	Dino Pepe
Director	Mario Crudo
Musical Director	Danny Johnson
Set Designer	Bruce Repei
Lighting Designer	Kirsten Watt
Costume Designer	Mervi Agombar
Stage Manager	Gillian Jones

It was subsequently produced, also in an earlier draft, at and by Ship's Company Theatre in Parrsboro, Nova Scotia, from August 3 to 28, 2011, with the following cast and company:

The Postmistress	Martha Irving
Pianist	Holly Arsenault
Saxophonist	Mitch Clarke
Director	Andrew Lamb
Musical Director	Holly Arsenault
Artistic Producer	Matthew Tiffin
Set and Props Designer	Andrew Murray
Lighting Designer	Paul Del Motte
Costume Designer	Krista Levy
Stage Manager	Ingrid Risk
Technical Director / Production Manager	Jonathon Harpur

It was produced in this, its final English version, by the Ode'min Giizis Festival at the Market Hall Performing Arts Centre in Peterborough, Ontario, from June 21 to 24, 2012, with the following cast and company:

The Postmistress	Patricia Cano
Pianist	Tomson Highway
Saxophonist	Marcus Ali
Director	Ruth Madoc-Jones
Musical Director	Tomson Highway
Producers	Patti Shaughnessy and Bill Kimball
Lighting and Set Designer	Ted Roberts
Costume Designer	Martha Cockshutt
Stage Manager	Elizabeth Kantor
Production Manager	Esther Vincent
Movement Coach	Marie-Josée Chartier

A French version, translated by Tomson Highway and Raymond Lalonde and titled *Zesty Gopher s'est fait écraser par un frigo*, was co-produced by the National Arts Centre and Théâtre du Nouvel-Ontario of Sudbury, Ontario, and performed at the NAC French Theatre in Ottawa from October 17 to 20, 2012, and in Sudbury from October 25 to November 3, 2012, with the following cast and company:

The Postmistress	Patricia Cano
Pianist	Tomson Highway
Saxophonist (Ottawa)	Vince Rimbach
Saxophonist (Sudbury)	Jean-Yves Bégin
Director	Geneviève Pineault
Musical Director	Tomson Highway
Translation Consultant	Robert Marinier
Set and Lighting Designer	Glen Charles Landry
Costume Designer	Isabelle Bélisle
Sound Designer	Frédéric St-Onge
Stage Manager	Marie-Josée Dionne
Movement Coach	Denise Vitali

SONG ORDER

Act One
    Taansi, Nimiss (Hey, Big Sister)
    Hey, Good-Lookin'
    Quand je danse (When I Dance)
    Oh, Little Bear
    Love I Know Is Here
    The Window

Act Two
    When I Was Last in Buenos Aires, Argentina
    Some Say a Rose
    Mad to Love
    Have I Told You
    The Robins of Dawn

THE (POST) MISTRESS

PRODUCTION NOTE

The (Post) Mistress is a two-act, one-person play about Marie-Louise Painchaud, a forty-nine-year-old francophone woman who grew up and lives in Northern Ontario.

The running time of the play is approximately 110 minutes, including one intermission.

SETTING

The post office in Lovely, a small town in francophone Northern Ontario.

Friday, August 9, 1986, that is, a time before the internet, when people wrote letters on paper, frequently by hand, and sent them by post.

SET

The first and main feature of the set is a wall completely covered with a gridwork of small, square aluminum boxes – the mailboxes, in effect, of a small country post office as seen from the back, from the perspective of the post-office workers who sort the mail. This, of course, is what the character Marie-Louise Painchaud will be doing throughout the play – sorting envelopes into these boxes. The second feature of the set is a counter that stands in front of the wall of mailboxes just off stage-centre toward stage left. This counter is seen not from the front, but from its left end only, so that the performer playing/working at this counter is never hidden by it but is plainly visible to the audience at all times. On top of this counter sit the paraphernalia of a postmistress, principal of which are a small pile of envelopes, evidently letters to be put into the mailboxes, and a desk bell. Other objects are optional, including a stapler and perhaps other post-office paraphernalia like a rubber stamp to cancel stamps. Under the counter, and thus not visible to the audience, lies concealed the box of checkers that will be needed as a prop as the show progresses.

Also not visible to the audience is a stairway painted black, away off at the back. The performer climbs this stairway when the time calls for it. At that time it should be outlined with twinkle lights so that it looks like she is climbing right up to the stars. The last feature of the set is a tombstone (optional) that stands to the side. Hollow and made of Plexiglas, it, too, remains invisible to the audience until the cemetery scene. At that time, it is lit from inside.

Off to stage right sits a black grand piano with pianist and, near him (or her), stands a saxophonist. In effect, they are the postmistress's "celestial orchestra." That is to say, if angels play harps in the standard image we have of heaven, in this heaven, angels play the piano and the saxophone.

A NOTE ON TRANSLATIONS AND PRONUNCIATION

Surtitles are projected against the wall of mailboxes (or against a backdrop) when translations are required. Speaking of which, because almost all the names for both people and places used in this text are Franco-Ontarian, every effort should be made to use their French pronunciation, for example, "Nicolah" in place of "Nicolas."

ACT ONE

*Silence. Darkness. Then we hear the voice of a forty-nine-year-old woman. It is **MARIE-LOUISE** Painchaud, the postmistress of the show's title, talking to a customer who, evidently, is just leaving the post office after doing some business with her.*

OFFSTAGE VOICE: Bernard Beaudoin? I can't marry you. You have a wife already. And a good one.

And the customer (Bernard Beaudoin) is gone, whereupon the woman (the postmistress) breaks into laughter, her laugh musical and lovely, like chimes in the wind. She laughs and laughs. And then talks to herself.

That Bernard Beaudoin. Always flirting when he comes in here to send his parcels. One of these days, he'll get himself into trouble, no doubt about it.

*She laughs again. And laughs and laughs. When the lights fade up, **MARIE-LOUISE** Painchaud, postmistress at the post office in Lovely, Ontario, a small farming community near the Northern Ontario mining city of Complexity, stands stage centre laughing and laughing. Attractive in her own way, she is, when all is said and done, your average housewife with, in her case, five grown or nearly grown children (none of whom, of course, we will see). She wears your standard Canada Post uniform of the period, rather nondescript yet well cut and thus rather elegant. In terms of character, she is one of those fun-loving, endlessly positive, and optimistic people who loves laughing, a person one loves to be with.*
As the lights come up, she is just finishing with another

1

customer – one, of course, we don't see as she (that is, this customer) has just left through the door.

MARIE-LOUISE: Monique Poirier, he should be baking a cake for you, not going out fishing for trout with his friends. It's your birthday, for God's sake. The next time that cornichon comes into my post office, I'll tell him to divorce you. Then we'll see who goes out fishing for trout.

> *And again, MARIE-LOUISE Painchaud bursts out laughing, this time, at her own joke. But the customer, at least, is gone now and she is alone. Then still chortling to herself, she takes some of the letters from the pile on the counter and starts sorting them into the mailboxes when, suddenly, she catches sight of the audience. Surprised, she stops in her tracks. At first, she is tongue-tied. Then she recovers from the surprise and starts talking to that audience.*

What are you doing here? (*Silence. No response.*) How long have you been sitting there watching me like that?

> *Pause. No answer forthcoming, she decides to play them for all they are worth. She smiles at them, an irresistibly charming mischievous smile, as though she is saying, "You want to know what I'm doing here? I'll show you what I'm doing here." And she starts speaking to them.*

Well, if you must know what I am doing here, I am putting these letters into these boxes.

> *MARIE-LOUISE stands up straight, fixes herself, clears her throat, and addresses the audience directly. (At some point*

*in her speech, she will pick up an envelope from the pile
on the counter.)*

Ahem. Marie-Louise Painchaud. Postmistress here in Lovely,
Ontario. You see this uniform, this counter, these boxes?
Mailboxes. This is a post office, my post office, the post office
where I work here in my hometown of Lovely, a small farming
town near Complexity, Ontario, and just spitting distance from
the legendary Rivière Armitage, the long and winding, cliff-
sided river that connects Lake Mahji-di-ate to Georgian Bay on
Lake Huron, so you can just imagine how beautiful it is, maple
trees for miles. You know of Complexity, of course. Copper-
mining city known for its penny the size of a church that sits
on a hill as you approach it from the west? Well, Lovely is one
hour east of Complexity. A village really. Population just two
thousand. I was born here, raised here. I've lived here all my
life. In fact, my ancestors here go back four generations to the
time my great-great-grandfather, Armand Boulanger, and his
wife, Hortense, came here as a newly married couple from
Alma, Quebec near Lac-Saint-Jean, to avoid starving to death
and when they got here – this was in 1860 – they gave birth
to fourteen children one of whom was my great-grandfather,
Lucien Boulanger who married a Cree Indian woman from
somewhere up north and played the accordion as did his
youngest granddaughter, my mother, Florence Poupette-née-
Boulanger. Me? I play the radio. And never been anywhere but
Complexity and Starlight Falls – and, once, even Ottawa, by
car – because, you see, I'm scared of flying. Forty-nine years
old, fifty come Christmas Day, and never been on an airplane.
Isn't that sad?

*In the background, a samba beat starts to play, infectious
and irresistible. Bizarrely enough, it seems to be coming
from inside an envelope that sits on the counter. Indeed,
the envelope itself seems to vibrate with samba. Hearing
the music, MARIE-LOUISE gets excited and moves toward
the envelope to pick it up. In a clandestine manner, she
addresses the audience as if she is telling them a
scrumptious secret.*

That's him. That's Barbaro Botafogo, my friend Sylvie
Labranche's secret lover, writing from Brazil, can you believe
it? He writes to her once a month ever since he had to fly back
home – after his term at the university in Complexity was over
one year ago – back to his wife and children in Rio de Janeiro,
Brazil, the sexiest city in the world, this Barbaro Botafogo tells
my friend Sylvie in these letters. Isn't that terrible? He has a
wife and God knows how many children down there and he
still writes to her, the nerve, but anyway. According to the man,
it's so hot down there in Rio de Janeiro that they wear nothing
but dental floss, even to go shopping. Ha! You wear dental floss
here in Lovely, Ontario, in February, and you'd freeze to death,
no doubt about it.

*The music having increased in volume, MARIE-LOUISE
starts singing, waving the letter this way and that as she
does, as if she's reading it through the envelope from
time to time.*

*MARIE-LOUISE sings "Taansi, Nimiss" / "(Hey, Big Sister)" to
the samba rhythm. The Cree words are sung without
Surtitle translations.*

(*singing*)

Taansi, nimiss,

Taansi, nistees,

Taansi! Kwayus

Nimithweetheeteenan

Eepeetootee-eek

Anooch kaatipskaak

Tanagaamooyaak

Taachimoostaatooyaak igwa

Meena

Tapaapiyaak, taneemee-itooyaak, hey!

Aastumik nitooteemuk, aastumik, hey!

Instrumental break. During the break, **MARIE-LOUISE**
resumes talking to the audience.

(*speaking*) He writes in Cree, can you believe it, this Barbaro
Botafogo? Because, you see, my friend Sylvie Labranche is
Métis – part Cree from Manitoba, part French from here – and
this Barbaro Botafogo is a ... a lingua, lingui ... something
or other whose specialty is aboriginal languages and who
came to Canada to study the Indians though, myself, I have
no idea why the Indians have to be studied, but anyway. This
Barbaro Botafogo speaks twenty languages, says my friend
Sylvie Labranche, can you believe it? Me, I speak two – French
and English – but him? Besides his native Portuguese and
his English, he speaks Chippewa, Chipewyan, Cherokee,
Choctaw, Chickasaw, Cheepoogoot, Chaggy-wat, Choggy-lat,
Chipoocheech, Chickadee, Chickabee, Chikamee, Chickalee,

Chickory, Chickaboom, Winnebago, Micmac-paddywhack-give-a-dog, and Cree, something like that. But Cree, for some reason, he tells Sylvie, is his favourite, can you believe it? "Cree, if you sing it to samba," this Barbaro Botafogo has said to my friend Sylvie Labranche, "sounds just like Brazilian Portuguese, same hot, sexy syllables," which is why he is obsessed by it (though if you ask me, if he is obsessed by anything, it is Sylvie Labranche, Métis princess who wears too much mascara). Still learning it, this Barbaro Botafogo is, according to Sylvie, from cassette tapes he copied at the Mahji-di-ate University library and from Sylvie. And how do I know this? Because my friend Sylvie Labranche reads them to me, right here in my post office when she opens them, reads them so often I might as well speak the language myself. I'll read it again, with translation this time.

> And **MARIE-LOUISE** goes back to singing, the very same
> thing she sang before, except that, this time, she translates
> each Cree phrase into English.

> (sings) *Taansi, nimiss,*
> (speaks) Hello, sister

> (sings) *Taansi, nistees,*
> (speaks) Hello, brother, is what those mean, in Cree.

> (sings) *Taansi! Kwayus*
> (speaks) "Hello, how much ..."

(*sings*) *Nimithweetheeteenaan*

(*speaks*) How much we like it ...

(*sings*) *Eepeetootee-eek*

(*speaks*) That you've come ...

(*sings*) *Anooch kaatipskaak*

      Tanagaamooyaak

(*speaks*) Tonight, we're gonna sing ...

(*sings*) *Taachimoostaatooyaak igwa*

(*speaks*) We're gonna tell stories and ...

(*sings*) *Meena*

      Tapaapiyaak, taneemee-itooyaak, hey!

(*speaks*) We're gonna laugh, we're gonna dance ...

(*sings*) *Aastumik, nitooteemuk, aastumik, hey!*

(*speaks*) So come, my friends, come, hey! That's what that
    means, in Cree!

Coda

(*sings*) *Aastumik, nitooteemuk*

(*speaks*) Yes, my friends, come!

(*sings*) *Aastumik, nitooteemuk, taansi, hey!*

End music. Finished singing, **MARIE-LOUISE** *resumes talking
to the audience.*

(*speaking*) "Barbaro Botafogo is preparing a speech for a Cree language conference in Manitoba and he needs my help getting it right," said Sylvie to me the other day at the Lovely Café next door to where she works. "He does?" I asked her, doubtful, because, you see, you never know with Sylvie Labranche, when she's serious and when she's not. (*aside, confidential*) Though if you ask me, she wears way too much mascara. Makes Tammy Faye Bakker look like a nun ... (*back to normal voice*) ... but anyway. Like, for instance, I am sure it has nothing to do with language conferences but with a plot she has hatched, in her mind, to sneak down to Brazil the first chance she gets there to whisper sweet nothings to the man in a language his wife will never understand. That's what she's like, that Sylvie Labranche. But he comes up to Canada to teach linguini at Mahji-di-ate University and study Native languages and look what he does, this Barbaro Botafogo: falls for a woman who files taxes at the municipal office here in Lovely and, on the side, collects hot men like some people collect those cute little teaspoons. But now he is back in his hometown waiting, I am sure, for Sylvie Labranche to come down from Canada and go prancing about on the beaches of Rio wearing nothing but mascara and dental floss.

> *MARIE-LOUISE turns her back to the audience, puts the letter into one of the mailboxes, then turns once more to the audience.*

You know, I've been working at this post office for thirty-one years. Started when I was eighteen years old. Sweet young thing I was back then. Not like now. Spilling out all over the place. It's a wonder this uniform doesn't explode. Fresh out of Complexity High I was. That bus ride, one hour there, one hour back, oh, but anyway. First job I had in my life, not as postmistress, of course, as I am today, but replacing the one person working here on his lunch breaks, Saturday mornings, when he was sick or playing hooky, that sort of thing. You gotta start at the bottom, my mother, Florence Poupette, may she rest in peace, used to say. But I stuck it out, worked and worked and worked and worked until, at age forty-one, eight years ago, I was made postmistress. That's when my predecessor, Jean-Marc Pilon, had a heart attack and died, right here on this counter while Antoinette Beaulieu was buying a money order from him. Boom. Dead. Oh, he was getting old anyway, a hundred years old, far as I was concerned, losing his marbles. Putting the wrong letters into the wrong boxes, charging people the wrong amount of money for sending parcels, that kind of thing. One time, he charged Gaston Godin, the tour boat operator at Carlton Bay, fifteen dollars for a single stamp, can you believe it? Gaston Godin just about had a heart attack but no, it was Jean-Marc himself who had it. Boom. Went up to heaven, he did, there to deliver mail to the angels, his widow, Therese – and I – sincerely believe. And, wouldn't you know it, but there was no one else in all of La Rivière Armitage area who had the qualifications. After all those years working behind Jean-Marc Pilon? Of course, I got the job. The first postmistress at the post office here in Lovely because, you see, everyone before me had been a ... well ... a ... just a post*master*. Hey, no one's perfect.

MARIE-LOUISE picks up another envelope from the pile on the counter and just keeps talking.

Now let's see. This one's for … (*She peers at the envelope.*) … Yvette Paquette. My, my. Yvette Paquette with her big hair. I don't care for the woman. A doctor's widow, so as wealthy as sin compared to the rest of us, yet raises not one finger for the church or the library but, then again, I'm not her favourite either but, hey. You can't win them all. She used to own a store in Complexity that sold tiles for bathrooms but is now retired here in Lovely aged fifty-five. Had an affair three years ago with that young man from New Orleans. Black guy, tall as a smokestack, thin as linguini. Drifted into Complexity from God-knows-where and stayed, setting off a wave of wild speculation and churning perplexity. Perplexity in Complexity, ha! Who is this man? was the question. And who does he take a shine to but Yvette Paquette – among others – and gets a job at the mine as a lift operator. Marly Fitzsimmons was what Yvette Paquette called him because he smoked Marlboros, those American cigarettes that kill people. (*looks at the envelope*) I knew it. Still in New Orleans where he went back to … to … (*whispers loudly*) They say he killed a man … (*back to normal voice*) … As if. (*Music starts. Sassy, butt-kicking Dixieland*) But never mind what he went back to. See the return address and the stamp? Birthplace, they say, of pork and beans with molasses and jambalaya and Louis Armstrong and jazz and all that stuff that that woman, Yvette Paquette with her big hair, is forever crowing about? And says Marly Fitzsimmons …

MARIE-LOUISE sings "Hey, Good-Lookin' " in Dixieland style.

(*singing*)

Hey, good-lookin', ain't you bookin'

Some nighttime nookin' with someone lookin'
About for come-what-may,
Say, just for time to play,
You look so, you look so
Fine you look so with it but so …
Unreadable,
Unfathomable;
Just imagine we'd play checkers,
Which I hear is good for neckers,
Or perhaps we could just gossip
Of rain or maybe of love.

Hey, looker, consider
What times we could concoct under
Conditions where,
Where one wouldn't dare
Not take it, not fake it,
Not make it work the way it would
Work for the best,
And all of the rest;
We'll play checkers just like neckers,
Then we'll turn the lights off, heckers!
Just consider, we could even
Fall in love!

*Instrumental break. During the break, **MARIE-LOUISE** talks to the audience.*

(*speaking*) See? If I hold it up to the light like this, I can sort of read it, ha-ha! He may have been a lift operator, that Marly Fitzsimmons, but he was known for something else. He was known for his ... his checkers. Oh, could he play? Whooo! Beat everyone, even Yvette Paquette, the best checkers player, at the time, in all of Complexity.

> *MARIE-LOUISE pulls out a box of checkers from under her counter and, as she continues speaking non-stop, opens it and sets the game up right there on the counter.*

Came with his own set all the way from New Orleans where they play checkers like neckers, he said to Yvette Paquette, and he'd walk into her house there on Polk Street up in Complexity, plunk himself down at her kitchen table, pull his checkers box out from under his coat, slap it down, and thus would begin the battle. Yvette Paquette would make the first move then fix her big hair, Marly Fitzsimmons would make the second and then they would pause and look at each other and then Yvette Paquette would eat one of his checkers and he'd eat one of hers, etc., etc., until Marly Fitzsimmons had eaten all of Yvette Paquette, I mean ... her checkers, and the board was left naked as sin and then Marly Fitzsimmons would reach over and turn off the lamp and, boom. Everything would be plunged into a darkness blacker than Satan and then God knows what would happen only Yvette Paquette with her big hair knows and she ain't telling! But now that this Marly Fitzsimmons is back in New Orleans seducing women left, right, and centre with a new set of checkers, he's sending her poetry describing the first time he played checkers with her, can you imagine?

> *And she sings.*

Hey, good-lookin', ain't you bookin'
Some nighttime nookin' with someone lookin'
About for come-what-may,
Say, just for time to play,
You look so, you look so
Fine you look so with it but so ...
Unreadable,
Unfathomable;
Just imagine we'd play checkers,
Which I hear is good for neckers,
Or perhaps we could just gossip
Of rain or maybe of love.

Hey, looker, consider,
What times we could concoct under
Conditions where,
Where one wouldn't dare
Not take it, not fake it,
Not make it work the way it would
Work for the best,
And all of the rest;
We'll play checkers just like neckers,
Then we'll turn the lights off, heckers!
Just consider, we could even
Fall in love!

Coda

We'll play checkers just like neckers,

Then we'll turn the lights off, heckers!
Just consider, we might even
Fall in love!

(*speaks*) Anybody out there wanna play checkers tonight?

*Boom. End music. Finished singing, **MARIE-LOUISE** talks to the audience.*

(*speaking*) That Yvette Paquette with her big hair, so easy to trick. Me? Impossible! For instance, Marly Fitzsimmons, seducer of women, came here with his checkers one day and you know what I did? Chased him out with my stapler. Without his checkers.

__MARIE-LOUISE__ shows the checkers to the audience, puts them back under the counter, turns around to put the letter into a mailbox, then returns to the audience.

Anyway, as the years went on and I'm working here at my post office handling mail all day, day after day. What happens? You become very good at it. You can do it blindfolded. And you see the same people come in here day after day, year after year. And they talk to you – they ask you for advice on this, advice on that. The number of marriages I've saved? Ha! And you begin to know all the details of their lives and, after a while, it's like you are the one who is living those lives and getting these letters from their secret lovers and their bankers and the Eaton's catalogue and the taxman and God himself, for all one knows.

She picks up another letter from the counter. Music starts, rubato intro. She reads the letter – through the

*envelope – with great effort, starting to sing as she does,
though at first, she sings in "free-form" only, with lots of
rubato, precisely because of the difficulty she is having
making out the words.*

*MARIE-LOUISE sings "Quand je danse" ("When I Dance")
largo, rubato, and then talks to the audience.*

Intro

    (*sings*) *Quand je danse ...*
    (*speaks*) Ach, this one's handwritten so it's hard to read.

    (*sings*) *Sous les étoiles ...*
    (*speaks*) But it's from that guy ...

    (*sings*) *Dans tes bras ...*
    (*speaks*) It's marked Montreal but ...

    (*sings*) *Oui, avec toi ...*
    (*speaks*) It's from that guy in Trois-Rivières ...

    (*sings*) *Je te regarde dans les yeux ...*
    (*speaks*) There's no return address, he's being
       mysterious ...

    (*sings*) *Et sais-tu ce que je vois ?*
    (*speaks*) Doesn't want anyone, including me ...

    (*sings*) *Ce que je vois dans tes yeux ...*
    (*speaks*) to know who it's from ...

(*sings*) *Est le reflet de ces étoiles et la lumière de ton amour ...*

(*speaks*) But no one fools Marie-Louise Painchaud,
     postmistress of Lovely, Ontario ...

(*sings*) *Donc ma belle ...*

(*speaks*) Oh, it's been so long since Roland – (*aside*) ...
     that's my husband – (*back to normal voice*) ... talked to
     me like this ...

(*sings*) *Viens me voir ...*

(*speaks*) About love, about chocolates ...

(*sings*) *Dansons bras sous bras ce soir.*

(*speaks*) All right, Roland? Tonight, whether you like it or
     not, we're gonna blame it on the bossa nova ... under
     the stars ..:

*An upbeat bossa nova rhythm begins. And now that we
are in the body of the song, **MARIE-LOUISE** sings
passionately.*

(*singing*)

Quand je danse sous les étoiles,

Dans tes bras, oui, avec toi,

Je te regarde dans les yeux,

Et sais-tu ce que je vois ?

Ce que je vois dans tes yeux,

Est le reflet de ces étoiles et la lumière de ton amour,

Donc ma belle, viens me voir,

Dansons bras sous bras ce soir.

[When I dance under the stars

In your arms, yes, with you, babe,

I look into your eyes

And you know what I see?

What I see in your eyes

Is the reflection of those stars and the light of your love,

So, my dear, come and see me,

Let us dance arm in arm tonight.]

Quand je pense éternité

Je ne vois que notre vie,

Quand je pense de permanence,

Je ne vois que notre vie,

Quand je rêve de notre amour,

Je ne vois que tes beaux yeux,

Et ton bon coeur et ta belle âme,

Donc ma belle, viens m'aimer, viens danser.

[When I think eternity

I see nothing but our life together,

When I think permanence,

I see nothing but our life,

When I dream of our love,

I see nothing but your beautiful eyes,

And your good heart and your beautiful soul,

So, my dear, come and love me, let us dance.]

Instrumental break. During the break, she talks to the audience.

(*speaking*) It's for that angry woman, Diane Gagnon, who came back to live, six months ago, at her mother's house on Doiron Road two miles east of Lovely. She left her husband and three children back in Trois-Rivières, Quebec. Bored stiff with being a housewife and cooking and cooking, she said. And in these letters, this poor husband, André Gagnon, taxi dispatcher, is trying everything in the book to get her to come back to him. But Diane Gagnon will have none of it. In fact, she told me to throw his letters into the garbage. As if. Still, I can sympathize with her because I, too, once left my husband, Rolly, because he would tell me off if he thought I hadn't done something properly. "But, Roland Painchaud," I would plead, "there's a kinder way of saying that, you don't have to hurt people to get your message across ..." and it would be over something as stupid as breaking the yolk on his breakfast egg or forgetting to wash his favourite shirt. So one day three years ago, I walked out with one suitcase. I left him with the three youngest kids we still had living at home, including – *mon dieu*, I was so selfish – my baby, Suzette, who was just nine. But I lasted one week and came back, though only after he'd sent me a letter at the Sapphire Motel in Starlight Falls where I was hiding, crying my eyes out. He'd found my refuge from that blabbermouth motel receptionist and, in that letter, he said the exact same thing as is being said here, thus winning me back, I swear by the beard of Roland Painchaud ...

> *The instrumental ended,* **MARIE-LOUISE** *resumes singing, reprising the second verse.*

> (*singing*)
> *Je ne vois que notre vie,*

Quand je pense de permanence,
Je ne vois que notre vie,
Quand je rêve de notre amour,
Je ne vois que tes beaux yeux,
Et ton bon coeur et ta belle âme,
Donc ma belle, viens m'aimer, viens danser.
[I see nothing but our life together,
When I think of permanence,
I see nothing but our life,
When I dream of our love,
I see nothing but your beautiful eyes,
And your good heart and your beautiful soul,
So, my dear, come and love me, let us dance.]

*By the end, she is in tears, tears of joy, tears of love, tears of nostalgia all mixed in together (for **MARIE-LOUISE** Painchaud, as you can tell by now, is a very emotional woman). End music. She talks to the audience.*

(*speaking*) That Diane Gagnon. I feel like driving down to her house – that is, her mother's house – on Doiron Road after my shift and telling her to go back to André.

She turns around, puts the letter into a mailbox behind her, and then returns her attention to the audience.

Because, you see, she comes here only after hours to pick up her mail, when the main part of the post office is closed but you can still get into the lobby and access the mailboxes from that side. This Diane Gagnon may have left Lovely twenty years ago but everyone still knows her and so she is scared, I am sure that people will ask her about her kids or, worse, about her husband. I would be, too, no doubt about it.

She sniffs, wipes away the last of her tears, and picks up another letter from the counter.

Oh dear, here's Michel St. Onge's one weekly letter. He gets them from his daughter, the one he lost to his wife, Pierrette. Another marriage from hell. What's with these people?! She runs off with a younger man – his wife, Pierrette, does – to Val-d'Or, Quebec, with their little girl. Married ten years only but they were fighting, he told me one day, Michel St. Onge did, at the liquor store where he works up on St. Joseph Street and where I was buying a bottle of Crown Royal for my husband, Roland. She said, this Pierrette did, that Michel didn't make enough money to support her and their kid, a girl who would be now – I'm guessing here – eight years old and cute as a button. According to the Complexity *Sun* – yes, the case actually reached the papers, splattered all over, pictures, everything, imagine! – according to the Complexity *Sun*, the little girl is not allowed to see her father because he got violent with his wife when he got drunk, in front of the girl, Pierrette said. In the papers! But she had expensive tastes, Michel said. In the papers! Furs, cars, shoes! And who, I ask, can afford shoes like Céline Dion on a liquor-store salary? And then she runs off with some sleazy truck driver! But this girl, Babette St. Onge ... (*Music starts in the background, a gentle waltz, a lullaby.*) ... eight years old, she writes to her papa every week from Val-d'Or, Quebec, sends him these poems she's written at school.

She begins singing. At one point during the song, the backdrop – maybe even the entire theatre – will start transforming into a starscape.

MARIE-LOUISE *sings "Oh, Little Bear."*

    (*singing*)

Verse 1

    Oh little bear, up in your sweet home,
    Pray do tell me, please,
    From high above this house,
    High above these trees,
    How starlight came to be,
    Your toy, your plaything, and
    How long you have been playing
    In such a wondrous land?
    How long you have been playing
    In such a wondrous land?

Verse 2

    Oh mother bear, up in your sweet den,
    Pray do tell me, please,
    From high above this land,
    High above this breeze,
    What lullabies you bring,
    To your sweet, dear, baby bear?
    Do you, at night's end, sing,
    "Oh, sleep my baby, fair?"

Do you, at night's end, sing,
"Oh, sleep my baby, fair?"

*Instrumental break. During the break, **MARIE-LOUISE**
addresses the audience.*

(*speaking*) It says, in this letter, that they went for a drive in
the country one day, this Babette St. Onge and her mother,
Pierrette, when, all of a sudden, a little bear ran across the road
in front of them. The little bear stopped, looked Babette directly
in the eye, smiled at her, and then disappeared into the bush.
But that night, Babette St. Onge says, this little bear came to
her in her dreams, down from the sky where he lives as the
constellation Little Bear, in French – Little Dipper in English –
came down from the sky to tell his friend, "Babette St. Onge,
your papa in Lovely is doing well but misses you." And then
the little bear's mother – that is, the Big Dipper – she came
down from her constellation to tell Babette – that is, Michel St.
Onge's daughter – "Come with me and I'll bring you to Lovely,
Ontario, to see your papa." And then, in this dream, Babette
St. Onge transforms into the Little Bear herself, up in the sky,
where her papa in Lovely can raise his eyes every night and see
her. And that's what Babette St. Onge, eight years old, says in
this letter ...

And she resumes singing.

Verse 3

The fourteen stars that give you both form,
In the sky so free,
Seven stars for mother,

Seven stars for baby,
The constellation of
Two creatures of the night,
While we here on this Earth,
Give thanks for such warm light.
While we here on this Earth,
Give thanks for such warm light.

*As coda, she hums the last two lines. End music. During
the course of the musical tag at the end of the song, the
starscape fades back into the wall of mailboxes and
MARIE-LOUISE herself is back behind her counter. She talks
to the audience.*

(*speaking*) You know, I live on the outskirts of Lovely, second-
last house on Pine Street, so just across from us is this field and
then this forest. And sometimes bears come into our yard at
night looking for food. Maybe next time I see a small one, I'll
call her Suzette ... ahm ... I mean ... Babette.

*She puts the letter into a mailbox behind her and picks up
another from the counter. Suddenly, she smells something
on it. A sensuous fragrance, one that makes her weak in
the knees. She raises the envelope to her nose. The letter
inside it laced with perfume, she takes a great long whiff,
the sensation so pleasurable she actually shudders.*

Nina Ricci. L'Air du temps. (*Then she snaps back to reality.*) Done
it again, that little bitch. Sprinkling perfume on these love
letters to ... to ... well, never mind to whom ... just to make
me jealous. Been living together, in sin, for twenty-five years,

that Daniel Dupuis and Guy Grandmaison, right there in their cottage on Lake Menard ten miles east of Lovely and they still write love letters to each other. A hairdresser and a policeman, imagine! In love for twenty-five years and they want me to know it because I have been married, legally, for twenty-five years to Roland Painchaud and I never get a letter – well, except that one time at the Sapphire Motel in Starlight Falls – but no letters sprinkled with his ... his Old Spice. And no flowers and no chocolates and, to add insult to injury, Daniel Dupuis is doing it again because they know that I have the most powerful sense of smell in all of La Rivière Armitage area, so powerful that it was once known to smell moose meat from ten miles away. And it's true, I get so jealous when one of these letters goes through my hands that I want to set it on fire except that there is a law against postal workers tampering with mail except in cases when they suspect ... a booby trap. Maybe I could do that, pretend that I'm suspecting it of being a letter bomb and call the police ... but no. Guy Grandmaison, Daniel Dupuis's man, is a cop. OPP. Ontario Provincial Police. Strong, muscles like ... He'd catch me lying and throw me in jail, no doubt about it. Imagine. Me, Marie-Louise Painchaud, postmistress of Lovely, Ontario? In jail? Ha! (*Music starts, a cool, jazzy country stride.*) So I just pretend they're for me, these words of love, written by my husband of twenty-five years. Roland Painchaud of Sainte-Rose-du-Lac, Manitoba, sitting at a table under his favourite maple tree writing and writing ...

And holding the envelope up toward the audience as to a window (for better light), she starts singing its words.

MARIE-LOUISE *sings "Love I Know Is Here."*

(singing chorus between each verse as indicated)

Chorus

It's one bright and sunny day,
The lake is smooth as glass,
The leaves of trees all green,
Birds are singing melodies,
The flowers are in bloom,
Such as you've never seen,
Sunlight streaming from the sky,
No, not a cloud in sight,
No rain today, it's clear,
Bells are ringing in my ears,
My heart is like a song,
Cuz love I know is here.

Verse 1

It was one bright sunny day,
July I do recall,
When I first saw the light,
I was walking through a park,
Kew Gardens was its name,
When I stopped for the flight,
Of ten chickadees at play,
Exploding from my heart,
A cloud of wondrous love,
Cuz it was inside that cloud,
You first appeared as though,

01341571936

25

HUMBER LIBRARIES

Descended from above.

Chorus

Chorus

    It's one bright and sunny day, etc. ...

Verse 2

    You said, "Hello, stranger," and
    Smiled one big sunny smile,
    And I said, "How are you."
    You walked up and told me birds
    Enchanted you so, and
    You dreamt of flying, too.
    We sat down upon that grass,
    Beneath that maple tree,
    Who whispered tenderly,
    As though telling us that time,
    Was perfect for us, and
    That we were meant to be.

    Instrumental break. During the break, **MARIE-LOUISE** *talks to the audience.*

(*speaking*) Daniel Dupuis tells me everything here in my post office and at the salon where I get my weekly perm. Some people, well, they're just like that. Me? When I'm alone here in my post office, which is quite often being as Lovely is such a small town, I'll smell these letters and hold them against my chest like this and feel the words and their perfume pierce through my skin and into my heart. "Rolly," I'll say to Roland at supper tonight, "how many years have you loved me and where, geographically, have you loved me and what have we done together all those years that tell me you love me? Have skies been sunny? Has there been rain or wind or cold?" And maybe he'll say ...

And she resumes singing.

Verse 3

> Twenty years and five it's been
> Together in the sun,
> The wind, the rain, the cold,
> Under clouds that threatened pain,
> Then gave way to the joy,
> Of laughter good as gold,
> Twenty years and five that seem,
> Like twenty minutes of
> A game so fine to play,
> Twenty years and five of love,
> And life with sunny skies,
> Of good times all the way.

Chorus

> La, la-la-la-la-la-la ... (*for the first half of the chorus only*)
> Sunlight streaming from the sky,
> No, not a cloud in sight,
> No rain today, it's clear,
> Bells are ringing in my ears,
> My heart is like a song,
> Cuz love I know is here.

Coda

> Bells are ringing in my ears,
> My heart is like a song,
> Cuz love I know is here,
> Love, love.

*End music. **MARIE-LOUISE** talks to the audience.*

(*speaking*) Oh, that Daniel Dupuis and Guy Grandmaison. Sometimes I love them. Sometimes I hate them. But they're happy. And how can you not be happy for people who are, eh? Even if they're two men living together. In sin.

> *She puts the letter into a mailbox behind her, takes another letter off the (dwindling) pile on the counter, and turns her attention back to the audience.*

Oh-oh. Here's one person who may be happy today but wasn't always. Rosa Lee Johnson, originally of Kirkland Lake, another small mining city, like Complexity, some two hundred miles northeast of here, but who has lived in Toronto all her life. Well, ever since she moved down there as a young girl of twenty. Never been back in Kirkland Lake since, at least not to live, her younger sister, Delma, tells me. Delma Burke, comes here once a week to sell me eggs from her chicken farm one mile past Daniel's Coiffure and pick up her mail and tell me her stories. But considering what happened to her elder sister, Rosa Lee Johnson, in Toronto all those years ago, you wonder why she, Rosa Lee Johnson, won't leave it. Still, today, she writes Delma these letters. So traumatized was she by the experience that she keeps writing the same story over and over like she ... she's frozen in time.

Music starts, a steel-hard, pounding bass, dark, ominous, dangerous.

More than six decades later, she still sees something inside the glass of a certain store window in Toronto. And no matter what Delma says to try to convince her to come and live up here with her, in her old age, she won't. Says it's that something that keeps her there. Love, I guess, will do that ...

MARIE-LOUISE sings "The Window."

(*singing*)

Verse 1

She was only twenty-something
When she took that silver bus
To the city where she met him
That man she would know as Gus;
She was said to have been shopping
For a brand new pair of shoes
When she paused outside one shoe store
To consider one pair that she might choose.

Chorus (to be repeated between each verse as indicated)

There reflected in the window
Stood a man of twenty-something;
How that boy would change her young life
All the heartache he would bring.

Verse 2

For five seconds she was daunted

She knew not how to react
For this boy did clearly want her
This her heart knew clear as fact;
Still her head did sort of warn that
Danger lurked upon his frame
But when she turned round to face him
Lover lips just handed her his name.

Chorus

There reflected in the window, etc. ...

Verse 3

Gus he told her was his first name
Cassidy his fama-lee,
Fixed car engines for a living
Born and raised in Bramalea;
She believed his every word then
Gave her name as Rosa Lee,
Rosa Lee Johnson from Kirkland.
She was lonely, so it seemed was he.

Chorus

There reflected in the window, etc. ...

Verse 4

Down the avenue they strolled then
Past the stores and all the bars
Under trees and by the flowers
Under skies with all their stars;

Hand in hand they lived for one year
Arm in arm for maybe two
Until one night he came home
Having drunk ten whiskies at The Brew.

Chorus

There reflected in the window, etc. ...

Verse 5

Lipstick on his collar some nights
Scent not worn by Rosa Lee,
She would find a letter on him
Penned by someone else not she;
He would slap her with his hand now
When she pleaded for his love,
He would tell her he loved her
Then attack her with one crunching shove.

Chorus

There reflected in the window, etc. ...

Verse 6

She would show up at work sometimes
Wearing purple, mauve, and blue,
Colours she would hide with makeup
Or sunglasses, Band-Aids, too;
Thus she'd stand behind the counter
At the Zellers at the mall,
Rosa Lee Johnson of Kirkland,

Broken armed, broken wristed, broken doll.

Chorus

There reflected in the window, etc. ...

Verse 7

Then one night he said he'd shoot her
With a gun he held in hand;
She just managed to evade him
With one question to demand;
In which second she grabbed something
Something sharp and made of steel,
She reached for his cold heart thus
She still dreams of the blood that she did feel.

Chorus

There reflected in the window, etc. ...

Verse 8

Now she's nearing eighty-something,
She still walks down avenues,
Past the bars and all the shoe stores
Selling shoes in all their hues;
She still pauses at that one store
To consider what to choose;
She still peers in that window
And then walks inside to buy her shoes.

Chorus

> (*repeat twice*)

> There reflected in the window, etc. ...

Coda

> (*singing*)

> All the heartache he did bring,

Music (and singing) comes to a smashing, atonal end. Freeze. Fade-out. During the fade-out, Rosa Lee Johnson's voice speaks out at us through the theatre sound system, steel-hard, bloodless, cold.

(*offstage voice of Rosa Lee Johnson*) Wipe that smirk off your face, you rat!

End of Act One

ACT TWO

Silence. Darkness. As the lights fade in, MARIE-LOUISE
Painchaud is just finishing sorting letters into mailboxes.
And humming to herself.

MARIE-LOUISE: (*speaking*) Daniel Bocquet, 24. Jane McCain, 57.
Labine's Meats and Variety, Jean-Marc's Pharmacy, Normand
Dube, 37, 78, 134, 18 ... Ahhh, from Argentina ...

The bass line of a tango snaps on. MARIE-LOUISE *freezes.*
As if the entire post office has been thrown into a time
warp by this address – and the rhythm that seems to be
coming from inside the envelope – time breaks down into
extreme slow motion so that, when MARIE-LOUISE *moves*
again, it is as if she is moving inside a dream, or under
water. The introduction to the tango builds up to full
formation – sensuous, dynamic, the piano eventually joined
by the saxophone playing winding, serpentine
configurations. Her eyes come up slowly to look at the
audience, a smouldering, come-and-see-me-I-dare-you sort
of look. And eventually, she starts talking (though, of
course, what she is doing is not so much reading as
"divining" the letter that she is holding). The moment she
starts speaking, time snaps back to normal, as do MARIE-
LOUISE's *movements.*

She recites "When I Was Last in Buenos Aires, Argentina."

(*speaking free-form over the rhythm of the tango*)

When I was last in Buenos Aires, Argentina,

That city of legend, city of love, *la ciudad del amor*

39

It was January, the height of summer, there, in Buenos
    Aires, Argentina,

So it was hot. Hot, hot, hot.

The sunlight was streaming, the people were steaming,
    I was steaming.

I was so hot, in fact, that I would have rosary beads of
    perspiration clinging to ...

Well ... just clinging. To ... *moi*.

Anyway, this, that, and the other

And this, that, and the other and, before you know it,

I end up in this neighbourhood called San Telmo

Where, as it turns out, the cool people live.

I look for an apartment.

I find an apartment

Which is where, and how, I meet this ...

This man named ... Ariel.

Ariel Juan Antonio Eduardo Pablo Augusto Alejandro
    Bellavista

That was his name but I called him just ... Ariel.

Ariel of the dark eyes, of the large flaring nostrils,

Thick purplish lips, swarthy complexion, very handsome.

The kind of man you see in Argentinian movies, the ones
    with what's her name there,

That famous Argentinian movie star who once acted with
    Eva Peron and hated her guts.

Libertad Lamarque, yes, that was her name,
    but anyway ...

We're not here to talk about Libertad Lamarque

We're here to talk about ... love ... *amor*

You see, I ended up renting an apartment from this ...

This Ariel Juan Antonio Eduardo Pablo Augusto Alejandro
    Bellavista

Whom I just called simply, as I say, Ariel,

Ariel of the dark eyes, Ariel of the large flaring nostrils,

Ariel of the thick purplish lips, of the swarthy complexion.

And that first night, he came up the stairs because, you
    see, he lived downstairs from me

And that first night, he came up the stairs

And he offered me ... *spagetti*. Not spaghetti but *spagetti*,

Spagetti with a hot red sauce, a sauce he himself had made

With herbs which, as he said, came from the jungles
    of Paraguay

Which is where his cleaning lady, Aricella, came
    from but ...

Anyway ... we had dinner that first night, on my terrace
    which was really his terrace

But I called it mine for the duration of my stay there

In Buenos Aires, Argentina, *la ville de légende, la ville
de l'amour*,

And we had dinner that night and we had many dinners
    thereafter ...

Him always coming up the stairs at the end of the day
   with his bowl of

Spagetti and me sitting there, on the terrace, with fresh
   red-hot lipstick

But because it was so hot, my lipstick would melt and the
   naked flesh of my lips

Would be exposed to the elements and ... Ariel ...

Ariel, he would look at my lips with

His eyes so deep and filled with a burning,
   mysterious light

As his *spagetti* would slide past those lips, into my mouth,

Over my tongue and down my esophagus,

And the people next door would be playing tangos

Tangos everywhere, absolutely everywhere in this city,

The city of legend, the city of love,

And before you know it, Ariel and I, we would be doing
   the tango ...

There, on my terrace, in the heat of the
   Argentinian summer

And he would hold me and I would hold him

He would hold me tenderly, I would hold him
   passionately,

And he would show me the most intricate movements,

Movements so complex, incredible, extraordinary,

Of my thorax, for instance, and of my arms and of ...

My legs, movements that I never knew my legs were
   capable of

At least up to that point in time.

One evening, he had me lifting them so high
    that, *mon dieu*,

I swore to God that

My dress would split right down the middle

And I would be exposed to the elements.

But elements or not, Ariel had a way of holding me

And throwing me around because, as you know,

The tango is the world's most violent dance,
    apart, perhaps,

From the lambada, it's true, but anyway ...

Ariel would throw me this way

And he would throw me that way

And he would throw me God-knows-where

And I would go flying

Toward the brick wall, for instance, of my terrace

And just as I was about to smash into it like a sack
    of potatoes

Ariel, who would have come chasing after me

On feet so light they were like a jungle cat's,

He would come chasing after me on tippytoes,

Catch me by one hand at the last split second,

Snap me around like a whip and bang me

Up against his chest so hard ...

Ah, his chest, his chest, his chest ...

I would see stars, in fact, one time I fainted

Not because of Ariel and his hairy chest but

Because of the heat, the heat of the Argentinian summer,

The heat of the southern hemisphere.

And we danced like that

All summer long, Ariel and I, on my terrace

In Buenos Aires, Argentina, city of legend, city of love,

Until I had to leave Buenos Aires, Argentina, at the end of
the summer

To go and see a man – another man – in Rio de Janeiro
but that's another story.

Another story for another day

But when last I was in Buenos Aires, Argentina,

The city of legend, the city of love, *la ciudad del amor*

It was the height of summer, there, in Buenos Aires,
Argentina,

And we would dance the tango, till five in the morning

Every morning, under the jacaranda trees, under the
stars with …

Ariel.

*For the coda, she wails to the tango rhythm. And wails and
wails, an improvised vocalise filled with a yearning, lyrical
nostalgia. End music. MARIE-LOUISE addresses
the audience.*

(*speaking*) That one was for my friend Marie-Luce St. Germain –
everyone in Lovely is my friend; well, except, perhaps, for

Yvette Paquette with her big hair, but anyway – Marie-Luce
St. Germain, the masseuse here in Lovely, getting a letter from
her friend Irene Latulippe a funeral director in Poppily-cum,
a lumber town some two hundred miles northwest of here.
You see, it seems this short, plump – and very adventurous –
Irene Latulippe went to Argentina recently and sent all these
letters about legs flying and lipstick melting ... well ... I got
to thinking ... why can't I do that? Why can't I, Marie-Louise
Painchaud of Lovely, Ontario, get over my fear of flying and
fly down to Buenos Aires, Argentina, and Rio de Janeiro, and
Lake Titicaca and have adventures like Irene Latulippe of
Poppily-cum without ... without my husband knowing. Roland
Painchaud, who has never bought me flowers or chocolates
let alone a plate of *spagetti*. That way I could be someone's
mistress, down there in Buenos Aires, Argentina, someone like
this ... this Irene Latulippe's Ariel Juan Antonio foom-foom-
foom ... Then come back up here to Lovely and Rolly a different
woman, at which point, I would be ... oh my God, I would
be a (post) mistress, wouldn't I? First, you see, I would have
been this Ariel's mistress, right? And then, because I would
have ditched him down there in Buenos Aires – "Maria Luisa
Pan-Caliente, please don't leave me," he would say, right there
in San Telmo. And I would say, "But Ariel, I have to go back
to my husband. And my children. In Lovely, Ontario." Boom.
End of story. Which would make me now, today, this Ariel's
postmistress. Oh, my God! I would be a real postmistress, a hot
postmistress, a scandalous, sinful, smouldering postmistress!
And why not? Cuz if you put me to the test, I, too, can throw
my legs into the air and melt my lipstick with hot *spagetti* and
bang my chest against men's hairy chests and split my skirt
right down the middle. (*Taking fright, she changes tone, abruptly*

loses all her passion.) Oh *mon dieu*, Rolly would kill me if he heard me talking like ... if he heard I was that kind of postmistress. He would lose it, no doubt about it. He would walk in that door, lift his moose-hunting rifle to his shoulder and, bang, get his target, for once, right on my forehead and I would fall on the counter like my predecessor, Jean-Marc Pilon, did that day. And don't think he won't, or can't, because my Rolly Painchaud, in fact, did do it one time. Or tried to. Drunk one night, he lost all his marbles and shot his wife's secret lover, or rather what he thought was his wife's secret lover, that is, my secret lover. Fortunately, he missed his target because he's always been a bad shot, thank God, worse when drunk. I mean, he once shot a moose in the head but got it in the rear somehow, right up that passage where the sun don't shine, poor moose. But there was no secret lover. As if. Imagine me, the wife of Roland Painchaud and the postmistress of Lovely, Ontario, with a secret lover. The truth is that he went and got drunk one night because he heard this story from that drunken snitch, Boom Boom Bedard, and went and shot at the wrong man. There was no man. It was his own long underwear hanging on the clothes line that he shot at. *That* was my secret lover.

So forget this story about Ariel in Buenos Aires, Argentina, and my split skirt. You see what these letters do to me? They upset me to the point where I have palpitations, to the point where I lose control of my emotions, I change personality, and become my clients. Maybe I've worked here too long. Maybe I should retire, collect my pension, and just go fishing. With Roland. Except that I am only forty-nine years old so forget it. I have easily another fifteen years to go.

She pops the letter into a mailbox and takes another from
the pile on the counter. Abruptly, the mood changes.

But they're not all funny, these letters. Sometimes, they bring bad news, of death, for instance, as this one does. This letter is from Josephine Maurice who went out west twelve years ago to work as a nurse and married a Cree man from there. Onion Lake, Northern Saskatchewan. Zesty Gopher, this man's name was, Cree sculptor famous for his statue of the Laughing Virgin in Saskatoon. And here, in this letter, Josephine – Fifi, everyone calls her – is describing Zesty's funeral to her family who still lives here in Lovely. Zesty Gopher, dead at thirty-nine, crushed by a fridge. Apparently, they were moving when the fridge? Falls from the truck, ka-chunk. Poor Zesty Gopher. And according to his widow, Fifi Gopher (née Maurice), she herself sang at his funeral and, as she sang … (*Music starts. Dirge-like in character, it is slow and stately, as for a funeral.*) … Zesty's mother, Pelagie Gopher, recited this prayer, in Cree, as her son's body was being lowered in his coffin to his final resting place. And Zesty's widow, Fifi, sang …

And she starts singing. Through the course of the song,
using lighting effects, we actually see **MARIE-LOUISE** *at the*
funeral singing this song first in the procession to the
cemetery then at the grave with its (optional) tombstone.
By the end of the song she is weeping.

MARIE-LOUISE *sings "Some Say a Rose."*
   (*singing*)
   Some say a rose has life for mere days only,
   They say it blooms and breathes then fades away;
   Some say a sparrow can ascend to heaven,

And that it sees from God's side down to men.
Some say that love has a life that can last for a day
Or a decade or three, even more;
Some say that life on this Earth has an ending that comes
When the human heart beats no more.

(*speaking*)

And Zesty's mother, Pelagie, prayed ...

Kinanaaskoomit'naan kaagithow keethawow

Ooma oota waaskeetuskameek ithigook kwayus

Kaagitaap'miyaak oomsi isi,

Meeg'waach oota eep'maat'siyaak.

[We thank you, all of you

Who on this Earth so very well

Watch over us in this way

While we live here.]

Kaagithow keethawow seetuk,

Waskwayuk, ooskaatigwuk, seetagwunaatigwuk,

[All of you trees,

birches, pines, spruce,]

Kaagithow keethawow pisisk'wuk

Mahiganuk, maageeseesuk, muskwuk,

Ateeg'wuk, amisk'wuk, atim'wuk,

[All of you four-legged creatures,

wolves, foxes, bears

caribou, beavers, dogs,]

Kaagithow keethawow pitheeseesuk,
Chaachaagathoowuk, peepeeks'eesuk,
Keeyaask'wuk, seeseepuk, mawg'wuk, migisoowuk,
[All of you creatures of the air,
blackbirds, robins
seagulls, ducks, loons, eagles]

Kaagithow keethawow neepeegaana, meensa, kinooseewuk
Assiniyuk, thootin, nipi, saagaa-iguna, aski.
[All of you flowers, berries, fish
rocks, wind, water, lakes, the Earth.]

Kinanaaskoomit'naan aski
Ithigook kwayus kaagana-ithimiyaak oomsi isi
Meeg'waach oota waaskeetuskameek eep'maat'siyaak
Ooma neet'naan ayut'sitinoowuk.
[We thank you, Earth,
for watching over us so well in this way
while we live here on this Earth
those of us known as humans]

Kinaanaskoomit'naan, kisaageet'naan,
Kinaanaaskoomitin, kisaageetin ...
[We thank you, we love you
I thank you, I love you ...]

(*singing*)

Some say that life on this Earth has an ending that comes

When the human heart beats no more,

Coda

When the human heart beats no more.

End music. Finished singing, **MARIE-LOUISE** *talks to the audience.*

(*speaking*) Oh, reminds me so much of the time when my husband – that is, my first husband, Winston Turner – died. Winner, we called him. Blue-eyed ray of sunshine. Only twenty-eight. Tourist-lodge manager. Boating accident, drowned on Lake Misty Maskimoot while out trout fishing, a storm. Leaving me a widow at age twenty-four, and single mother to a toddler and a baby. Marie-Louise Painchaud – at one time Mary Lou Turner – of Lovely, Ontario. Postmistress, in a sense, to the dead Winston Turner, late manager of the Carlton Bay Lodge. So then I waited two years after his funeral, which I thought was a respectable period of time, before I looked at other men. Which is when I met Rolly. Roland Painchaud, carpenter and contractor, builder of houses, builder of that, all-round handyman. Big strapping guy recently arrived in Starlight Falls from Sainte-Rose-du-Lac, Manitoba. Bumped into him at the Safeway store in Starlight Falls, literally, with my shopping cart, him rushing around the corner with an armful of canned goods and crackers and cereal in boxes. Comes rushing around the corner and, boom, crashes right into my shopping cart, drops all his groceries. So I bend down to help him pick them up and he says, "No need." But I help anyway and before we know it, we're reaching for the same can of beans and we're touching, hands, fingers ... and that was it, boom, the spark was lit. No doubt about it. At first, we were young and foolish, even with my children, both preschoolers at the time, whom he willingly adopted, God bless the man. He himself had never been married. It was later that it became a rough-and-tumble situation when our little family had grown to five kids in total and I had to keep working. Which is when I left him. August the ninth, 1983, his birthday of all days, raining and raining. I went and hid out at the Sapphire Motel in Starlight Falls. Thank God I was on holiday that week. (*Music starts. Berlin-style cabaret, hard and driving, hypnotic.*) Now this is not me in this letter – it's from Bernadette Couture to her on-again, off-again husband, Marcel Couture. Always a dresser – four-inch heels, flame-red nails – she now lives in Montreal working at Eaton's in retail, apparently, but she's originally from Complexity and he, Marcel Couture, moved back here, his hometown, to take over his father's business repairing outboard motors. They might still get together and fix their marriage. Who knows? But the story in this letter might as well be me and Rolly three years ago ...

> *At this point, the free-form pattern of her speech*
> *transforms into "Berlin cabaret rap" – hard and driving,*
> *unrelenting, mean, like a locomotive – yet, somehow, sexy*
> *as hell. (NOTE: Musical keys are shown for each verse to*
> *guide musical directors and musicians.)*
>
> *She recites "Mad to Love."*

(speaking with emphasis as shown in italic)

Verse 1

Twas a *Sat*urday at *eight* [Am]

In the *morn*ing in the *spring*,

It was *rain*ing in the *yard*,

It was *rain*ing on the *Kings*way,

Verse 2

I was *walk*ing down the *street*, [Dm]

I was *walk*ing down the *road*,

My *um*brella in my *hand*,

My e*mo*tions in the *mode*

Verse 3

Of at*tempt*ing to en*joy* life, [G7]

*E*ven with the *rain*,

Of at*tempt*ing to enjoy *life*,

*E*ven with the *pain*,

Verse 4

Of the *ang*er in my *heart*, [C]

Of the *ang*er cuz you *see*,

You had *spok*en bad of *us*,

You had *spok*en bad of *me*,

Verse 5

Why? [A7]

Why oh why oh *why* oh why oh,

Why oh why oh *why*?

I ain't gonna *lie*,

Verse 6

Cuz you *say* I been *boss*in' you [Dm]

A*round* I been *push*in',

Been *act*ing with a *lack* of,

Con*sid*eration *for*,

Verse 7

Re*spect* for *you*, [G7]

Cuz *cer*tainly re*spect*,

Is *some*thing you know *not* of,

Is *what* you say to *me*,

Verse 8

Is *what* you said to *me*, [C]

As *we* were having *cof*fee,

First thing in the *mor*ning,

You *look*in' right at *me*,

Verse 9

So *what* was I to *say* and [Am]

What was I to *do*,

Save for *tel*ling you that *you*,

Gotta *lit*tle problem, *too*,

Verse 10

What are you ex*pect*in' [Dm]

I'm *gon*na sit there like a *fool*,

Take it in the *face* then

Go and play at *pool*? Ha!

Verse 11

You *got*ta be *kid*din' me, [G7]

You *got*ta be a *fool*,

Cuz the *last* thing on my *mind*,

Was to *go* out playing *pool*,

Verse 12

Cuz *list*en here my *friend* and [C]

*List*en to me *well*,

I'm *gon*na take a *min*ute here,

A *sto*ry you to *tell*,

Verse 13

'Bout a *doz*en years a*go*, [A7]

Per*haps* two *doz*en,

I'm *sorr*y my *mem*ory

Is *not* what it *was* then,

Verse 14

But a *do*zen years a*go*, [Dm]

You were *sitt*in' in a *bar*,

I was *sitt*in' in a *bar*,

And you *said* to me, "How *are* you?"

Verse 15

I was *flum*moxed by the *fact* [G7]

That a *stran*ger would *ad*dress me,

As *if* he might have *known* me,

As *if* he might as*sess*,

Verse 16

My e*mo*tional rea*li*ty, [C]

I was *take*n quite a*back*,

But I *clev*erly con*cealed* it,

And de*ci*ded to at*tack*,

Verse 17

I de*ci*ded to at*tack* [E7]

With my *ar*senal of *charms*,

That *put* you right at *ease*,

Where you *o*pened up your *arms* where,

Verse 18

You *o*pened up your *brain* [Am]

And you *o*pened up your *heart*,

And you *told* me you were *hur*tin',

Were *fall*in' right a*part*,

Verse 19

Your *love* had been re*jec*ted, [D7]

Your *love* had been ab*used*,

Your *life* was in a *funk*,

And *you* were not a*mused*,

Verse 20

"How *could* you be a*mused*?" [G7]

I *said* to you right *there* and then,

I *would*n't be a*mused*,

Then I *lis*tened till e*lev*en,

Verse 21

Yes, *we* were there for *hours*, [E7]

*May*be three or *four*,

One *beer* after a*noth*er,

You *moved* me to the *core*,

Verse 22

You had *giv*en her a *chance*, [Am]

You had *giv*en her a *car*,

You had *cov*ered all the *bills*,

*E*ven from a*far*,

Verse 23

When *you* were on the *road*, [D7]

Playing *mu*sic in the *bars*,

You had *give*n her a *house*,

You had *give*n her the *stars*,

Verse 24

Yet *first* chance she *got*, [G7]

She *threw* you in the *dirt*,

You were *an*gry, you were *achin'*, [C]

You were *hurt*!

(*singing*)

Chorus A

You were hurtin', [Am]

You were sad,

You were cryin', [Dm]

You were mad,

I consoled you, [G7]

I was sad,

I embraced you, [C]

I was mad,

(*singing*)

Chorus B

Mad to take you, [A7]

Mad to love,

Mad to hold you, [Dm]
Mad to love,
Inside my heart, [G7]
Mad to love,
Mad to love you, [C]
Mad to love ...

*Instrumental break in which the musicians play the form
from verse 17 to verse 24. During the break, **MARIE-
LOUISE** mimes the actions described so that, in effect, she
is living out the scene: walking in the rain in a trench coat
while carrying an umbrella. She acts out her anger to the
saxophonist who, in a sense, becomes her husband in the
story (the saxophonist, of course, is busy playing and
doesn't respond). The instrumental ends and **MARIE-
LOUISE** resumes her rap.*

(*speaking*)

Verse 25

So *then* I took a *look* [E7]
At a *fu*ture we might *share*,
And *kind*a live to*ge*ther,
*Kind*a form a *pair*,

Verse 26

We *dat*ed for a *week* and we [Am]
*Dat*ed for a *year*,
We *dat*ed for a *long* time,

You *call*ing me a *dear*,

Me *call*ing you a *sweet*heart, [D7]

Me *call*ing you a *dove*,

You *call*ing me a *sweet* pea,

You *call*ing me my *love*,

Took you *right* into the *core*, [G7]

Of *my* old *heart*,

My own *life*,

Fell *right* into the *part*,

Of *lov*in' wife and *part*ner, [E7]

I *cooked* up all the *meals*,

And *washed* the dishes *after*,

Ne*go*tiated *deals*,

Where you *got* a better *job*, [Am]

Where you *got* better *pay*,

While I *cov*ered all the *bills*,

And that's *all* I have to *say*,

Verse 31

> Cuz you *star*ted talkin' *ill*, [D7]
>
> Of the *man*ner I ap*pear*,
>
> You *star*ted talkin' *ill*
>
> Of the *man*ner I make *love*, dear,

Verse 32

> You *acc*used me of this *crime*, [G7]
>
> You *acc*used me of that *crime*,
>
> You in*formed* me I was *cheat*in',
>
> For no *rea*son or no *rhyme*,

Verse 33

> So I'm *out* here in the *rain*, [C]
>
> My *um*brella in my *hand*,
>
> Ain't *that* just *grand*?
>
> Grand!

*For a coda, she trails off with either an improvised scat or an insane, wailing vocalise, sort of reminiscent of the coda for "When I Was Last in Buenos Aires." End music. **MARIE-LOUISE** goes back to her regular, conversational voice.*

(*speaking*) But then again, what marriage, what relationship doesn't go through such phases? Sometimes you're so madly in love, it hurts physically; some days you could care less. But you know what? We hung in there and we hung in there like a couple of dirty shirts, me and Rolly, up, down, up, down and, little by little, these last three years especially, the ups started outnumbering the downs and things started gelling. Sometimes it takes some huge crisis or other to change life for the better but ... if you're patient and think not only of yourself but of the other person and, of course, the kids, and you keep working at it, then things eventually do settle down. (*She slides the "Mad to Love" letter into a mailbox and takes another one – the second last one – from the pile on the counter.*) Genevieve Trudeau, country-piano player ...

> *Music for a slow romantic ballad begins to play.*

... for The Tremblay Brothers, who got back from their tour not quite in time to say goodbye to her as she lay dying ... leukemia. There at Complexity General. Genevieve Trudeau, thirty-two years old – blonde, tall, willowy – on her deathbed, dictating, barely, to a nurse this letter to Christian Tremblay, saxophone player and my cousin ... Christian himself swears he dreamt these words ...

> **MARIE-LOUISE** *sings "Have I Told You."*

> (*singing free-form with plenty of rubato*)

Verse 1

> (*sings*) Have I told you that I miss you when you're gone ...
> (*speaks*) Oh, these love letters, they always make me cry.

> (*sings*) For a day or for an hour, just a while ...
> (*speaks*) I mean, cry inside myself, not outwardly, I'm
> not that bad.

(*sings*) I lie sleepless ...

(*speaks*) If I did, cry outwardly.

(*sings*) feeling lonely ...

(*speaks*) I'd be a mess, I'd lose my job.

(*sings*) From one end of endless night up to the dawn ...

(*speaks*) Oh, Rolly, Rolly, Rolly ...

(*sings, now al tempo, a slow, romantic ballad*)

When the morning comes I walk out to the sea,

And I stand there gazing out at silver spray,

And I ask her if she meant that we be one heart, one soul,
then how can this be?

Chorus

You're away now but you're with me, please convince me,

Please convince me that you'll come back to me softly,

By the time night takes her sky back and envelops us
both gently.

Verse 2

Have I told you how I feel about the life

That you've given me to live here by your side,

Crying sometimes, laughing some but ever thoughtful of
each other and that life,

When you wake up in the morning like a dove,

When you lie there by my side deep in the night,

I pray always, I know always that the angels watch upon
us from above.

Chorus

> You're away now but you're with me, please convince me,
>
> Please convince me that you'll come back to me softly,
>
> By the time night takes her sky back and envelops us
>> both gently.

*Instrumental break. During the break, **MARIE-LOUISE** talks to the audience.*

(*speaking*) You know what, dear friends, my dear Lovely people? I forgot to tell you something. I forgot to tell you something rather important. I forgot to tell you that ... I'm dead. (*The music stops cold. Silence for eight whole seconds. Then ...*) Yes, I died ten months ago, from breast cancer. (*Music starts again. She resumes speaking.*) As you know, too many women die of breast cancer at age forty-nine. For women, that seems to be the year. Plucked from the Earth like roses at the most beautiful point in their lives, when they are about to enter their years of wisdom. That's what helped smooth things out between me and Rolly. It was when, at age forty-six, they found the cancer. On me. It didn't take long did it? Just three years from the time I was diagnosed to the time I died. But when I left Rolly to go and hide out at the Sapphire Motel in Starlight Falls that time? I ran away not because I'd broken the yolk on his breakfast egg or forgot to wash his favourite shirt. I mean, who runs away from a broken egg yolk? The real reason was the diagnosis that I'd gotten just three days before. The news. It hits you like a sledgehammer, *mon dieu, mon dieu,* but ... those last three years of our lives, me and Rolly ... and our children: Jerome, now twenty-seven; Natalie, twenty-five; Michel-Marc, eighteen; Rene, fifteen; Suzette, just twelve – those years, they were the best ...

And she sings.

Coda

> Have I told you that I love you in the night,
>
> Have I told you that I love you in the day,
>
> And I'll always, I will always for so long as stars exist and shine their light.
>
> And I'll always, I will always ...
>
> Have I told you that I love you,
>
> Have I told you ...

*End music. In the silence that ensues, **MARIE-LOUISE** turns around to slip the letter into a mailbox, then talks to the audience.*

(*speaking*) So now that I'm dead – I mean, why do you think I can read letters through their envelopes? Ha-ha, tricked you, didn't I?! – now that I'm dead, I work in this great big post office up here in the sky handling mail between the dead and the living, letters they send to each other through their dreams – the human dream as the ultimate postal system: imagine! – an endless river of dreams that passes through these hot little hands of mine, so I'm very busy as you can see. And why do these dreams always have to pass through my hands as opposed to going directly from the dead person up in heaven to the living person down on Earth? Because I, Marie-Louise Painchaud, am the (post) mistress. Always was, always will be. It's my job, my calling, my raison-d'être. And while I work here, I wait for Rolly to join me. And I hope I have to wait until he's at least ninety years old. That's another forty years. For me? Up here? That's seconds. For him? Down there? A long time. And the kids, Jerome, Natalie, Michel-Marc, Rene, and Suzette, my baby, only twelve years old, I hope ... I hope that they all have many grandchildren and great-grandchildren. (*She yells down to "Earth."*) I want five hundred of them little munchkins, do you hear me, Suzette Painchaud? (*back to normal voice*) And I hope ... I hope that the world survives another ten generations, at least – a hundred generations – and I hope that people will stop hurting each other and learn to laugh. And laugh and laugh and laugh, like this ...

> *She laughs one last time, a lovely, lovely laugh that rings and rings and rings, echoed to gigantic proportions on the theatre sound system. Ideally, it should crescendo to the point where it is like thunder that paralyzes us all for an entire eight seconds. Incredibly haunting, it is obvious that it comes from another world entirely. Then she reads the address on the last envelope.*

From Catherine Pharand ... (*Music starts, an anthem, a hymn of praise.*) ... to her husband, Jean-Pierre Pharand, late dairy farmer, who rests at the cemetery down there in Lovely just across the street from my (post) post office. And she, at age ninety and kindness incarnate, may now live at the Mapleview Retirement Home in Ottawa, but every year on his birthday, she sends him this letter, care of me, and through it, she wishes him a happy birthday. So this year, for the first time by dream post, it's "Happy ninety-third, Jean-Pierre from your loving wife, Catherine," as you lie there in your grave away down there in Lovely serenaded by ...

She starts to sing. Eventually, she will be singing, literally, at Pierre's grave, the tombstone now fully lit from its interior.

MARIE-LOUISE sings "The Robins of Dawn" as she would a hymn or anthem.

(*singing*)

Verse 1

    The robins of dawn
    Are singing a song,
    So lovely you dream,
    Of singing along;
    The happy thing being,
    The language they're singing,
    These creatures with wings,
    Is one you are learning.

    Ces arbres devant nous,
    Ils chantent une chanson,
    Si jolie, si belle,
    C'est quoi leur raison ?
    Oui, tu te demandes,
    Même si ton corps sait,
    Qu'ils chantent dans une langue,
    Que ton coeur connait.
    [These trees before us,
    They're singing a song,
    So pretty, so beautiful,

What is their reason?

Yes, you ask yourself,

Even if your body knows,

That they sing in a language,

That your heart knows.]

Chorus

They're singing a song,

To wish you much happiness on this Earth,

They're wishing you health,

They're wishing you peace and love and great mirth;

They're singing a song,

To wish you a happy birthday and may

You sing your sweet song,

For many a long, fine day.

Instrumental break. During the break, **MARIE-LOUISE**
addresses the audience one final time.

(*speaking*) When I was alive, I would cross the street after work
every August the seventh – just two days before my own Rolly's
birthday, imagine – to go to the cemetery down there in Lovely.
And I would sit there on that stone bench and read this letter
for Catherine Pharand to her husband there in his grave. Did
it for ten years. And now that my own grave is there right next
to Jean-Pierre's, I can just prop myself up on one elbow, turn
to the white-haired old thing, and tell him directly. But that's
just my body inside that coffin because my spirit, my soul? It's
up here in the sky just a-working merrily away in my heavenly
post office. The only thing missing is that the love of my life,

Roland Painchaud, is not yet with me. I mean, I'm happy to be postmistress to the dead and the living but that's not enough. Something is missing. For it's only when he joins me up here – because, you see, my first husband, Winston Turner, being Anglo, has to stay on the Protestant side of heaven, and I, as a francophone *and* a Catholic, can go there only on Tuesdays, so I need my Rolly – it's only when Rolly joins me up here that I can let go. Of earthly life. So I can be whole, so that, finally, I will be *post* postmistress to the living. So Roland Leonard Painchaud, my love, mon amour, today, August the ninth, 1986, here's a letter coming, by dream post, from me to you ...

And she sings, just belts it right out to a smashing finish.

Verse 2

The wind in the trees,
Is singing a song,
So awesome you think,
Of singing along;
The lucky thing being,
The language she's singing,
This creature with lungs,
Is one you are learning.

MARIE-LOUISE *begins climbing the stairs.*

Ooma n'si aski,
Taatoo geesigow,
Maana nagamoo,
Kinsitootawow na?

Noosisim, wanskaa,

Maana kaa-itisk,

Nigoosis, aastum,

Maana kaa-itisk.

[Look at this Earth,

Every day,

How she sings,

Do you understand her?

My grandchild, awake,

She says to you,

My son, come to me,

She says to you.]

Chorus

They're singing a song,

To wish you much happiness on this Earth,

They're wishing you health,

They're wishing you peace and love and great mirth;

They're singing a song,

To wish you a happy birthday and may

You sing your sweet song,

For many a long, fine day.

Coda

May you sing your sweet song

For many a long, fine day.

*End music. Freeze. Having climbed up to "the stars" during the last part of her song, **MARIE-LOUISE** Painchaud now stands in "the sky" holding up a letter to read its address in* *the fading light of day. The starscape fades in one last time to cover the entire stage (if not the entire theatre). And with it, this time, appears its newest, its most recent constellation, the (Post) Mistress. Freeze. Slow fade-out. And one last time, in that fade-out, we hear **MARIE-LOUISE**'s voice coming to us not from this world but from "beyond" (that is, on the theatre sound system), a celestial, silvery, miraculous voice, a voice Roland Painchaud now hears nightly in his dreams.*

(*speaking*) Don't forget to pick Suzette up at the library on your way home, Rolly, my love ...

END

ACKNOWLEDGEMENTS

The author owes his deep and heartfelt thanks for the development of this play to those people and organizations listed in the production credits as well as to the following: Ruth Madoc-Jones, for dramaturging and coaxing, lovingly, the text into its (next to) final form; Raymond Lalonde; Michèle Surroca; Robert Marinier; Kate Mensour; Geneviève Pineault; Brigitte Haentjens; Maureen Labonté; the Banff Centre Playwrights Colony; Le Théâtre du Nouvel-Ontario; Jean-Yves Begin; and Alexie Lalonde-Steedman, who produced the cabaret of the very first showing of the songs in this text on the nights of August 7 and 8, 2009, at Le Théâtre du Nouvel-Ontario in Sudbury, Ontario.

ABOUT THE AUTHOR

Tomson Highway is a writer from Northern Manitoba. His best-known works are the plays *The Rez Sisters*, *Dry Lips Oughta Move to Kapuskasing*, *Rose*, and *Ernestine Shuswap Gets Her Trout* as well as the best-selling novel *Kiss of the Fur Queen*. He writes in three languages: Cree (his mother tongue), French, and English. As a classically trained pianist (who also writes music), he has studied with some of the finest teachers in Canada, most notably William Aide and Anton Kuerti.

0 1341 1571193 6